'S WONDE

George & Ira Gershwin's™

BROADWAY SHOWSTOPPERS

Editor: Tony Esposito

ISBN: 0-89724-591-1

CONTENTS

THE BABBIT AND THE BROMIDE	*FUNNY FACE*	47
BIDIN' MY TIME	*GIRL CRAZY*	88
BUT NOT FOR ME	*GIRL CRAZY*	91
BY STRAUSS	*THE SHOW IS ON*	123
CLAP 'YO HANDS	*OH, KAY*	31
DO IT AGAIN	*THE FRENCH DOLL*	4
EMBRACEABLE YOU	*GIRL CRAZY*	95
FASCINATING RHYTHM	*LADY, BE GOOD*	16
FIDGETY FEET	*OH, KAY*	35
FUNNY FACE	*FUNNY FACE*	52
HE LOVES AND SHE LOVES	*FUNNY FACE*	56
HIGH HAT	*FUNNY FACE*	60
HOW LONG HAS THIS BEEN GOING ON?	*ROSALIE*	72
I GOT RHYTHM	*GIRL CRAZY*	99
I'LL BUILD A STAIRWAY TO PARADISE	*GEORGE WHITE'S SCANDALS 1922*	8

Love is here to stay
Love walked in
They can't take that away from me

CONTENTS

ISN'T IT A PITY	*PARDON MY ENGLISH*	111
I'VE GOT A CRUSH ON YOU	*STRIKE UP THE BAND*	80
LIZA	*SHOW GIRL*	76
THE MAN I LOVE	*LADY, BE GOOD*	20
MINE	*LET 'EM EAT CAKE*	116
MY ONE AND ONLY	*FUNNY FACE*	64
OF THEE I SING	*OF THEE I SING*	103
OH, LADY BE GOOD	*LADY, BE GOOD*	24
'S WONDERFUL	*FUNNY FACE*	68
SOMEBODY LOVES ME	*GEORGE WHITE'S SCANDALS 1924*	12
SOMEONE TO WATCH OVER ME	*OH, KAY*	39
SOON	*STRIKE UP THE BAND*	84
STRIKE UP THE BAND	*STRIKE UP THE BAND*	43
SWEET AND LOW-DOWN	*TIP-TOES*	27
WHO CARES?	*OF THEE I SING*	107

DO IT AGAIN!

Words by
B.G. DeSYLVA

Music by
GEORGE GERSHWIN

Cm6 D7 Gm Cm6 D7
I was-n't snug-gl-ing, You should know I real-ly was strug-gl-ing
G7 Dm7 G7 Dm7 G7 C7
rall.
I've on - ly met you, And I should - n't let you, but
rall.
Refrain
In slow fox-trot time
p-mf F F6
Oh, do it a - gain,
p-mf
Fma7 F F6 F+ F Dm
I may say, "No, no, no, no, no," But do it a - gain.

G7 Edim G7 Cdim C7 D7 Gm7 C7
My lips just ache to have you take, The kiss that's
cresc.
Bb F Cm6 D7 G7
wait-ing for you. You know if you do,
C rit. C Gm Cdim C7 a tempo F
You won't re-gret it, come and get it. Oh,
rit.
a tempo
F6 Fma7 F F6 F+
no one is near, I may cry, "Oh, oh, oh, oh,

F Dm G7 Edim G7 Cdim
oh," But no one will hear
Ma - ma may
C7 D7 Gm7 Cm6 D7
scold me 'cause she told me It is naugh - ty, but then,
cresc.
G7 rit. Bbm C7
Oh, do it a - gain,
Please do it a - gain!
rit.
1. F D9 C9 C7+5 2. F
a tempo
f
3
pp

I'LL BUILD A STAIRWAY TO PARADISE

Words by
B.G. DeSYLVA and IRA GERSHWIN

Music by
GEORGE GERSHWIN

F7 Bb A7 Ab7 G7 F#7 F7
Of the dance that car - ry you through The gates of Heav - en
fz
Bb F#7 B
It's mad - ness To be al - ways sit - ting a - round in sad-ness
G7 C Ab7
When you could be learn - ing the steps of glad-ness You'll be hap-py when you can
Db C7 B7 Bb7 A7 Ab7 G G7-5
do just six or sev - en Be - gin to - day! You'll

G7sus4 G9 C G+5 C G+
find it nice The quick-est way to Par - a - dise
E A B7 Em C°7 G7
When you prac-tice Here's the thing to do Sim-ply say as you go.
Refrain Con spirito
p-f C G7 C7 G
I'll build a stair-way to Par - a - dise With a new step ev - 'ry
p-f
C7 F C7 F7
day! I'm going to get there at a - ny price Stand a -

Em7 C F♯°7 G7sus4 G7 C
-side I'm on my way! I've got the blues And up a-
A♭7
-bove it's so fair Shoes! Go on and car-ry me there!
C G7+5 C7 C♯°7
I'll build a stair-way to Par-a-dise, With a
D7 G7sus4 G7 1 C F♯°7 G7 2 C A♭7 C
new step ev-'ry day. day.

SOMEBODY LOVES ME

Words by
BALLARD MACDONALD and B.G. DeSYLVA
French version by EMELIA RENAUD

Music by
GEORGE GERSHWIN

Am7 D7 sus G D7 G7 Em Cm6 D7 Em Em6
Heav - en's pret - ty pro - gram for we've nev - er met; I'm
Du des - sein des cieux car je ne l'ai trou - vée; Je
Bm Bm6 E7 Em7 A7 D7 D+
poco rit.
clutch - ing at straws, just be - cause I may meet her yet.
veux es - pé - rer qu'un jour je la ren - con - tre - rai.
Refrain
G (molto legato)
a tempo
p-f
Am7 Am D G
Some - bod - y loves me I won - der
Quel - qu'un m'ai - me - ra Je ne sais
p-f a tempo
C7 G C7 Am7 D7
who, I won - der who she can be;
qui Mais c'est un fait é - ta - bli

G D7-9 G
Some - bod - y
Quel - qu'un m'ai -
Am7 Am D7 G A7
loves me I wish I knew,
me - ra Je veux sa - voir,
Bm C♯7-9 C♯m7 F♯7 Bm
Who can she be wor - ries me,
C'est ce qui fait mon sou - ci,
E7 Am Dm6 Am Dm6
For ev - 'ry girl who pass - es me I shout, Hey!
Pour cha - que bel - le qui pas - se je cris Oh!

Am
may - be,
la! la!
Em7 A7 Em7 A7
You were meant to be my lov - ing
Se - rait el - le par ha - zard mon
D7 D+
ba - by;
a - mie?
G Am7 Am D7
Some - bod - y loves me
Quel - qu'un m'ai - me - ra
G C7
I won - der who,
Je ne sais qui
3
G Em Am7 D7
May - be it's
Peut - ê - tre
1. G D7
you.
vous
2. G Am G
you.
vous.
mf
rit. e dim.
ff

FASCINATING RHYTHM

Music and Lyrics by
GEORGE GERSHWIN
and IRA GERSHWIN

E♭7 E♭m B♭m F7 sus.4 B♭m E♭7 B♭m B♭m7
out an-y warn-ing, And hangs a-round all day. I'll have to sneak up to it,
mf
cresc.
E♭ E♭m F7 B♭
Some-day, and speak up to it, I hope it list-ens when I say:
REFRAIN
B♭7 A♭ B♭7 A♭ B♭7 A♭ B♭7 A♭ B♭7 A♭ B♭7 A♭
"Fas-ci-nat-ing Rhy-thm You've got me on the go! Fas-ci - nat-ing Rhy-thm I'm all a -
p
B♭7 E♭ D♭ E♭7 D♭ E♭7 D♭ E♭7 D♭
qui - ver. What a mess you're mak-ing! The neigh-bors want to know why I'm

E♭7 D♭ E♭7 D♭ E♭7 A♭ Fm7 Gm B♭+5 9
al-ways shak-ing Just like a fliv-ver. Each morn-ing I get up_with the
E♭ E♭7 Cm E♭6 B♭+ F E♭dim.
sun, (Start a hop-ping nev-er stop-ping) To find at night, no work_has been
B♭7 C♯dim. B♭7 A♭ B♭7 A♭
done. I know that once it did-n't mat-ter But
B♭7 A♭ B♭7 A♭ B♭7 A♭ B♭7 A♭ B♭7
now you're do-ing wrong; When you start to pat-ter, I'm so un-hap-py.

E♭7 D♭ E♭7 D♭ E♭7 D♭ E♭7 D♭ E♭7 D♭ E♭7 D♭
Won't you take a day off? De - cide to run a-long Some-where far a-way off, And make it
E♭7 A♭ Fm6 G7 Cm B♭ E♭ma.7 F7
snap-py! Oh, how I long to be — the man I used to be!
mf
B♭7 A♭ B♭7 A♭ B♭ F7 B♭7
1. E♭
Fas-ci-nat-ing Rhy-thm, Oh, won't you stop pick-ing on me!"
p
E D C B
2. E♭ A♭ Cm E♭ Fm A♭ E♭
me!"
mf cresc. sf

THE MAN I LOVE

Music and Lyrics by
GEORGE GERSHWIN
and IRA GERSHWIN

E♭ B♭7 Gm Cm6 Cdim
though I re - al - ize as well as you, It is sel - dom that a dream comes true,
B♭ F7(♭9) B♭ B♭dim A♭ B♭7
To me it's clear That he'll ap - pear.
dim.
poco rall.
Refrain (slowly)
E♭ E♭m B♭m
Some-day he'll come a - long, The man I love; And he'll be big and strong,
p molto semplice e dolce
C7aug5 Fm7-5 B♭7
The man I love; And when he comes my way, I'll do my best to

Eb Abmaj.7 Gm Bb7 Eb
make him stay. He'll look at me and smile,
p
Ebm Bbm C7aug5 C7
I'll un-der-stand; And in a lit-tle while He'll take my hand;
Fm7-5 Bb7 Bb7(sus) Bb7(6) Eb Ebmaj.7 Ab
And though it seems ab-surd, I know we both won't say a
Eb Adim Ab7 G7 Cm Cm7 D7 Ddim Cm
word. May-be I shall meet him Sun-day, may-be Mon-day, may-be
mf poco espr.

G7 Cm Cm7 D7 Ddim Cm Gdim
not; Still I'm sure to meet him one day, May - be Tues - day will be
poco rit.
Ab Bb7 Eb Ebm
my good news day. He'll build a lit - tle home, Just meant for two,
dim.
p a tempo
Bbm C7aug5 C7 Fm7-5
From which I'll nev - er roam, Who would, would you? And so all else a - bove,
1. 2.
Bb7 Fm7 Bb7 Eb Ab6 Eb Bb7 Eb
I'm wait - ing for the man I love. love.
mp
p

OH, LADY BE GOOD!

Music and Lyrics by
GEORGE GERSHWIN
and IRA GERSHWIN

E F#m7 B7 E A E F#7 B7 E D7
I could blos - som out I know, With some - bod - y just like you, so,
If some - bod - y won't re - spond, I'm go - ing to end it all, so,
p
mf
rit.
Refrain: G D7 G C7 G G#o D7
p - mf slow and gracefully
Oh, sweet and love - ly la - dy, be good! Oh la - dy, be good
Oh, sweet and love - ly la - dy, be good! Oh la - dy, be good
p - mf
G D7 G C7
to me! I am so aw - f'ly
to me! I am so aw - f'ly
G G#o D7 G
mis - un - der - stood, So la - dy, be good to me.
mis - un - der - stood, So la - dy, be good to me.

G7 C D7 C G D7
Oh, please have some pit - y,
This is tu - lip weath - er
mf molto espress.
Em B+ Em A7 Am7 D7 Em Am7 A7-5 G D7 G
I'm all a - lone in this big cit - y. I tell you I'm just a
So let's put two and two to - geth - er. I tell you I'm just a
p
C7 G G#o D7
lone - some babe in the wood, So la - dy, be good to
lone - some babe in the wood, So la - dy, be good to
1. G D7 Am7 D7
me!
2. G C7 G
me!

SWEET AND LOW-DOWN

Music and Lyrics by
GEORGE GERHWIN
and IRA GERSHWIN

Am7-5
dim.
D7
Gm7
D9
Gm
They crave noth - ing else but the low down there If you need a ton - ic,
dim.
p
Cm
A7
D7
rit.
C
Fm11
D7
And the need is chron - ic; If you're in a cri - sis, My ad - vice is:
molto cresc.
rit.
Refrain:
G
p - f a tempo
cresc.
Grab a cab and go down To where the band is play - ing; Where
p - f a tempo
cresc.
G#o7
D
Eb
E
milk and hon - ey flow down, Where ev - 'ry - one is say - ing, "Blow
mf

Dm7 D7+5 G6 Eb7 G
p
that Sweet and Low-Down!" (tu - tu!) Bus - y as a bea - ver, You'll
dance un - til you tot - ter; You're sure to get the fe - ver For
G#o7 D Eb E Dm7 mf D7+5 G6
noth - ing could be hot - ter, Oh, that Sweet and Low - Down!
B7
mp
Phi - los - o - pher or dea - con, You sim - ply have to weak - en.

E9sus4 E7 E9sus4 E7 E7sus4 (+9) A9 E7sus4 (+9) A9 Am9 D9
Spoken:
Hear those shuf - fling feet! — You can't keep your seat! — Professor!
mf
Am9 C9 G
p
Start your beat! — Come a-long! Get in it! You'll love the syn - co-pa - tion! The
p
G#o7 D Eb E Dm7 Am7 D7
min - ute they be-gin it, You're shout - ing to the na - tion: "Blow that Sweet and
1.
G Em Bm Am9 D
Low - Down!"
2.
G Eb9 G
Low - Down!"
3
sf
Ped.
*

CLAP YO' HANDS

Music and Lyrics by
GEORGE GERSHWIN
and IRA GERSHWIN

Gm7 C7 F Bm7-5
with the dance that you do.
mf
marcato
Am E7 Am Fdim. A E7 A A7
Let me lead the way; Ju - bi - lee to - day.
mp
Dm A+5 Dm7 G A7+5 Dm G7 C7
He'll nev - er hound you, Stamp on the ground, you chil - dren! Come on!
p
REFRAIN
F C7 F
Clap - a yo' hand! Slap - a yo' thigh! Hal - le - lu - yah! Hal - le -
p - f

C7 F7 B♭ B♭7 B♭6 D♭m6 C7 F
lu-yah! Ev-'ry-bod-y come a-long and join the ju-bi-lee!
mf
F+5 F C7 F
Clap-a yo' hand! Slap-a yo' thigh! Don't you lose time, don't you
p
C7 F7 B♭ B♭7 B♭6 D♭m6 C7 F
lose time, Come a-long, it's shake yo' shoes time now for you and me!
G7 C Fm F Fm C C7
On the sands of time you are on-ly a peb-ble;

Fmaj.7 B♭ B♭m C+5 C7+5 Fm
Re-mem-ber, trou-ble must be treat-ed just like a re-bel,
C7 F C7 F
Send him to the deb-ble! Clap-a yo' hand! Slap-a yo' thigh! Hal-le-lu-yah! Hal-le-
C7 F7 B♭ B♭7 C7
lu-yah! Ev-'ry bod-y come a-long and join the ju-bi-
1. F D♭7 C7
lee.
2. F B♭ F
lee.

FIDGETY FEET

Music and Lyrics by
GEORGE GERSHWIN
and IRA GERSHWIN

Gm
C7
B♭
PHIL
F7
B♭
I need no phi - si - cian. What can it be?
Fm7-5
mf POTTER
C♭7
p PHIL
F7
un poco rit
You can help me out. What's it all a - bout?
mf
p
un poco rit
B♭7
Refrain
POTTER
p-f a tempo.
I've got fidg-et-y feet, fidg-et - y feet, fidg - et - y
p-f a tempo.
C7
feet! Oh, what fidg - et - y feet, fidg - et -

C
Fm7
-y feet, fidg - et - y feet! Say, mate,
B♭ B♭7 E♭ E♭m G G+ Em G
mf
come and be my sway mate; How can an - y -
G+ Em G G+ D7 G F♯m
one re - sist that rhyth - mi - cal beat?
Fm B♭7
You will nev - er go wrong, nev - er go wrong, nev - er go
p

B♭7
E♭7
mf
wrong, If you tod - dle a - long, tod - dle
mf
A♭Maj7
A♭
a - long, tod-dle a - long. All I need's a part - ner to make
E
E♭Maj7
G7
piu f
C7+5
Fm7
B♭7
my life com - plete, Two more fidg - et - y, fidg - et - y
piu f
1
E♭ E♭7
F7
B♭7 C7
Fm6 C♭7
2
E♭ A♭7
B♭7+5 E♭
feet.
feet.
f

SOMEONE TO WATCH OVER ME

Music and Lyrics by
GEORGE GERSHWIN
and IRA GERSHWIN

Eb Ebmaj7 Eb9 Eb7 Abmaj7 Cm
Look - ing ev - 'ry-where, Have - n't found him yet; He's the big af - fair I can -
F7 Fm7 Gm Bb7 Eb Ab
not for - get. On - ly man I ev - er Think of with re - gret.
Eb D7(b9) Gm C Gm
mp
I'd like to add his i - ni - tial to my mon - o - gram.
C7 Bb Bb6 Cm7 F7 Bb Ab Gm Bb7
mf
un poco rall.
Tell me, where is the shep-herd for this lost lamb?

Eb
a tempo
p
Eb7 Ab6 Abo Eb Ebo Bb7 Bbo
There's a some - bod - y I'm long-ing to see. I hope that he Turns out to be
p a tempo
Fm C7 Fm Am7-5 Fm7 Bb7 Eb G7+5 Ab Bb7 Eb Eb7
Some-one who'll watch o - ver me. I'm a lit - tle lamb who's
p
Ab6 Abo Eb Ebo Bb7 Bbo Fm C7 Fm
lost in the wood. I know I could Al-ways be good To one who'll
Am7-5 Fm7 Bb7 Eb Eb7 Ab Bb7 Eb Ab
watch o - ver me. Al - though he may not be the
mf

Eb D7 D7+5 D7 G7
man some Girls think of as hand-some. To my heart he car-ries the
C C7 F7 Bb7 Eb Eb7 Ab6 Abo
key. Won't you tell him please to put on some speed,
p
Eb Ebo Bb7 Bbo Fm C7 Fm Am7-5 Fm7 Bb7
Fol-low my lead, Oh, how I need Some-one to watch o-ver
1. Eb Eb7 Ab G7+5 Fm7 Bb7+5
me.
2. Eb Eb7 Ab Abm Eb
me.
mf
mf

STRIKE UP THE BAND

Music and Lyrics by
GEORGE GERSHWIN
and IRA GERSHWIN

Ab Bbm Fm C7 Fm C7 F C7
oth - er war But if we are forced in - to one The flag that we'll be
F Bb F C7 F F7 Bbm Ebm
fight - ing for, Is the Red and White and Blue One! We do not fa - vor
molto marcato
Bb7 Ebm Bbm Cm7 Bbm Fm C7-5 F7 Bbm
rall.
war a - larms, Rum - ta - ta - tum - tum - tum! But if we hear the
rall.
Cm7 Bbm Eb9 Bbm Fm Gbmaj7 F
call to arms, Rum - ta - ta - tum - tum, Rum - ta - ta - tum - tum, Rum - ta - ta - tum - tum - tum!

Refrain:
very marked
(Spoken)
(Imitation of Trpt.)
F7 Bb Bb6 Bb B°
Let the drums roll out! Let the trum - pet call! While the
(Boom boom boom!) (Ta - ta - ra - ta - ta - ta - ta!)
mf - f
(shouted)
F7 Bb Ab Bb7 Cm
peo - ple shout! Strike up the band! Hear the cym - bals ring!
(Hoo - ray!)
(Spoken) (Trpt.) (Shouted)
Eb E° Bb7
Call - ing one and all To the mar - tial swing
(Tszing - tszing - tszing!) (Ta - ta - ra - ta - ta - ta - ta!) (Left,
Eb Cm7—5 Bb Bb6
Strike up the band! There is work to be done, to be
Yan - kee Doo, Doo - dle - oo, Doo - dle -
right!)

Bb Eb Ebmaj7 Am D9 Am D7 Gm C9
done! There's a war to be won, to be won! Come, you son of a son of a
oo, We'll come through, Doo-dle-oo, Doo-dle-oo, For the red, white and blue, Doo-dle-
Gm C7 F7 Bb
gun! Take your stand! Fall in line, yea bo! Come a-
oo, Lend a hand! With our flag un-furled, For a
Dm7 G9 G7 Cm7 Gm Eb6 Em7–5 F7sus4 F7
long, let's go! Hey, lead-er! Strike up the
brave, new world! Hey, lead-er! Strike up the
1. 2.
Bb G C F7 Bb
band! Let the band!
L.H.
R.H.
sf sf

THE BABBIT AND THE BROMIDE

From "Funny Face"

Music and Lyrics by
GEORGE GERSHWIN
and IRA GERSHWIN

No Chord
p
F♯7
They both were sol - id cit - i - zens they
That they had both de - vel - oped in ten
A harp each one was car - ry - ing and
ff
p
E♭7
F♯7
both had been a - round, And as they spoke you clear - ly saw their
years, there was no doubt, And so, of course, they had an aw - ful
both were wear - ing wings, And this is what they said as they were
A7
NC
feet were on the ground.
lot to talk a - bout;
strum-ming on the strings;
ff
sffz

Refrain
D7 G D7 G C/D G D7
p p-mf
1. "Hel - lo! How are you? How - za folks? What's
2. " " ditto
3. " " ditto
p p-mf
G C/D D7 C/D D7
new? I'm great! That's good! Ha - ha! Knock
sempre stacc.
G D7 G D7 G C/D G C/D
wood! Well, well! What say? How - ya been? Nice
G C/D D7 C/D D7
day. How's tricks? What's new? That's fine! How are

G
B7
you Nice weath - er we are hav - ing but it
I'm sure I know your face, but I just
You've grown a lit - tle stout - er since I
Em
B7
gives me such a pain; I've tak - en my um -
can't re - call your name, Well, how've you been old
saw you last, I think; You must come o - ver
Em A7 D7 G D7
mf
brel - la, so of course it does - n't rain. 1. Heig - ho! That's
boy? You're look - ing just a - bout the same. 2. ditto
some - day and we'll have a lit - tle drink. 3. ditto
f
mf

G C/D G C/D G C/D D7 C/E
life! What's new? How-za wife? Got to run! Oh,
D7 G C
my! Ta-ta! Ol-ive oil! Good-bye!
DANCE
fz
tr
G D7 G D7
marcato
1-2 G B7 Em
3 G
sf
ff
D.S.

FUNNY FACE

Music and Lyrics by
GEORGE GERSHWIN
and IRA GERSHWIN

Gsus4 Gm Dm Gm Em7-5 C9 Cm7-5 Bb F7
peals to me, please, don't think I've sud - den - ly gone
Cit - y, dear, Miss A - mer - i - ca I'd nev - er
Bb Bb7 Gb Db6 Gb
mad. You have all the qual - i - ties of Pe - ter Pan,
be. Truth to tell, though, you're not such a lot your - self,
Db7 Gb Bb7 Eb Am7-5
I'd go far be - fore I'd find a sweet - er pan. I
as a Paul Swan you are not so hot your - self. And yet I
Refrain:
p-mf
Bb7 Am7-5 Bb7 F9 Bb7 Bb7+5
love your fun - ny face, your
love your fun - ny face, your
p-mf

Eb Ab7 Eb Cm
sun - ny fun - ny face, for
sun - ny fun - ny face. You
F7 Fm7 Bb7 6 Bb7+5
you're a cu - tie with more than beau - ty, you've
can't re - pair it, so I de - clare it is
Eb Bbmaj13 Bb7+5 Gm7-5 C9 F7
got a lot of per - son - al - i - ty N. T. A
quite all right. He: Like Ron - ald Col - man? She: So's your ol' man!
dolce
Bb7 Am7-5 Bb7 F9 Bb7 Bb7+5
thou - sand laughs I've found, in
Yet it's ver - y clear, I'm

Eb7 Dm7-5 Eb7 Ab7
hav - ing you a - round.
glad when you are near.
Ebmaj7 Bb7 Gm7-5 Eb
Though you're no Glo - ria Swan - son, for
Though you're no hand - some Har - ry, for
Ab Cm7 F7 Bb7 Am7-5 Bb7 Bb7+5
worlds I'd not re - place your sun - ny fun - ny
worlds I'd not re - place your sun - ny fun - ny
1.
Eb Cm9 B11 Bb11 Eb B7 Bb11 F9
face. I
2.
Eb Abm Eb Ab9 Eb
face.
f
p

HE LOVES AND SHE LOVES

Music and Lyrics by
GEORGE GERSHWIN
and IRA GERSHWIN

Abmaj7 Ab6 Abmaj7 A°7 C F7-5
full of hap - py fac - es, It's be - cause they
Em7 C Dm7 G7 C D7 Gm7 C9
rall. e dim.
all love That won - drous thing they call love.
colla voce
Slowly, with sentiment
Refrain:
F C9 Am7-5
p - mf
He loves and she loves and they love, So
p - mf
D+ D7 Gm7 Gm7-5 C C7 F Dm7
why can't you love and I love, too?
scherzando

Gm7 C7 F C9 Am7-5
Birds love and bees love and whis - per - ing
D+ D7 Gm7 Gm7-5 C C7 F Bm7-5 B♭7
trees love, And that's what we both should do.
Am7 A♭m6 Gm7 C7 F7 C7 F9
Oh, I al - ways knew, some day
B♭6 F7 B♭ B♭6 D7
you'd come a - long; We'll make a

Am7-5 D7 Gm Gm7 C7 Gm7 rit. C7
two - some that just can't go wrong, hear me:
rit.
F a tempo C9 Am7-5
He loves and she loves and they love, So
a tempo
D+ D7 Gm7 Gm7-5 C C7
won't you love me as I love
why can't you love and I love,
1. F G9-5 F7 Bb Gm7 C C7
you.
f
2. F G9-5 F
too?
f

HIGH HAT

Music and Lyrics by
GEORGE GERSHWIN
and IRA GERSHWIN

F C7 F Em7-5 C7
He: No use step - ping out that way, the thing to do is lay low;
Gm Gm7 F Fmaj7 Gm Gm7 F E7+5
you can't win by treat - ing her as if she wore a ha - lo.
Am E9 Am E7sus4 E7
Chorus:
What is your so - lu - tion? Tell us if you can.
Am E9 Am Dm7 Gm9
He: Here's my con - tri - bu - tion to man: High

Refrain:
p-f
F
Bb
C7
hat!
You've got to treat them high hat!
Don't let them know that you care;
F7
Bb
Gm9
C9
F
D7
but act like a frig - id - aire,
you'll win
ad lib.
C^7_6
Gm7
Bo7
Eb
them like that.
Stand pat!

Bb
Gm7-5
Put on your gay - est cra - vat,
Fmaj9
Bb
C7
but keep your feet on the ground.
fz
F
D9
C7/6
Oh boy! How they'll come a - round!
Just treat them high
1.
F
Dm7
G9
C7
2.
F
C7+5
F
hat!
High
hat!
f
sfz

MY ONE AND ONLY (What Am I Gonna Do)

Music and Lyrics by
GEORGE GERSHWIN
and IRA GERSHWIN

Am C C+ Am Em7 Am F♯o7
my cards are on the ta - ble.
of tak - ing me for grant - ed.
C7 F F+ Dm F♯o7
There must be lots of oth - er men you hyp - no - tize.
And if you cared you should have told me long a - go;
C7 F G♭maj7 G7 F7
rall.
All of a sud - den I've be - gun to re - al - ize as fol - lows:
dear, oth - er - wise, how in the world was I to know? Oh, lis - ten:
Refrain: Cm7-5 F7 Cm7-5 F7
p-mf a tempo
He: My one and on - ly, what am I gon - na do if you turn me down,

Cm7-5 Eb7 F7 Bb6 Bb Bbm
When I'm so cra - zy o - ver you?
espressivo
mf
3
Cm7-5 F Cm7-5 F
p
I'd be so lone - ly, where am I gon - na go if you turn me down?
p
3
Cm7-5 Eb7 F7 Bb6 F Bb F7
Why black - en all my skies of blue? I tell you
espressivo
Bb Bbmaj7 Bb7sus4 Eb7
mf
I'm not ask - ing an - y mir - a - cle; it can be done! It
mf

Ebm Bb Bbmaj7 Bb7sus4
can be done! I know a cler - gy - man who will grow lyr - i - cal
Eb7 Gb9 F7 Cm7-5 F
and make us one, and make us one. So my one and on - ly, there
p
p
Cm7-5 F Cm7-5 Eb7 F7
is - n't a rea - son why you should turn me down when I'm so cra - zy o - ver
3
3
espressivo
1.
2.
Bb Bo F7 Bb Ebm Bb
you!
you!
mf
mf
sf

'S WONDERFUL

Music and Lyrics by
GEORGE GERSHWIN
and IRA GERSHWIN

'S Wonderful - 4 - 1

Cm Eb Am7-5 D7 Gm Bb7+5 Gm7-5 C7
How can words ex - press Your di - vine ap - peal?
When you said you care, 'Mag - ine my e - mosh;
Fm C Fm7-5 Bb Eb Bb Bbo C7
You can nev - er guess All the love I feel.
I swore then and there Per - ma - nent de - vosh.
Bb F9 F7 Bb Dbm6 Gb7
From now on la - dy I in - sist,
You made all oth - er boys seem blah;
Bb F9 F7 Fm7 Abm Bb7
un poco rit.
For me no oth - er girls ex - ist.
Just you a - lone filled me with Aah!
un poco rit.

Refrain:
Eb
p - mf a tempo
Eb6 Eb Eb6 C7 C#o C7 C#o
'S won - der - ful! 'S mar - vel - ous!
p - mf a tempo
Bb7(add6) Bb7 Eb6 Eb Eb6 Eb Eb Eb6
You should care for me! 'S aw - ful nice
Eb Eb6 C7 C#o C7 C#o Bb(add6) Bb7
'S par - a - dise! 'S what I love to
Eb6 Am7-5 G D
see! You've made my life so
My dear, it's four - leaf
mf

G
D7
Dm6
cresc.
C7
glam - or - ous
clo - ver time,
You can't blame me for feel - ing
From now on my heart's work - ing
cresc.
F7
Bb7
pEb
Eb6
Eb
Eb6
am - o - rous.
o - ver - time.
Oh! 'S won - der - ful!
p
mfCm
F
Fm7
p
E°
Fm7
Bb7
'S mar - vel - ous! That you should care for
mf
p
1.
Eb
Gm
Fm
Ab
Gm
Cm
Fm7
Bb
2.
Eb
Ab
Eb
me!
me!
mf
mf

HOW LONG HAS THIS BEEN GOING ON?

Music and Lyrics by
GEORGE GERSHWIN
and IRA GERSHWIN

A7 Em7 A7 Am D7
mf
So, my dear, I swore,__ "Nev - er, nev - er - more!"__
Dar - ling, can't you see__ 't'was for char - i - ty.__
mf
G Em7 Am7 D7 G Em7 G
p
On my list I in - sist - ed that kiss - ing must be crossed out.__
Though these lips have made slips, it was nev - er real - ly se - rious.__
Bm E9 C#7 F#7-5 F#7-9 Bm Bm7 Bo7
mf
Now I find I was blind, and oh la - dy, how I've lost out!__
Who'd a'thought I'd be brought to a state that's so de - li - rious?__
mf
Refrain:
D7 Do7 Bb D7 D7+5 G7 C7 Cm7
p-mf
I could cry__ salt - y tears;__ Where have I been all these years?__
I could cry__ salt - y tears;__ Where have I been all these years?__
p-mf

G Go Am7 D7 G7 C D7
Lit - tle wow, tell me now how long has this been go - ing on?
Lis - ten you tell me do how long has this been go - ing on?
G D7 Do7 Bb D7 D7+5 G7
p
There were chills up my spine, and some thrills I
What a kick! How I buzz! Boy, you click as
C7 Cm7 G Go Am7 D7 G7
can't de - fine. Lis - ten sweet, I re - peat: How
no one does! Hear me sweet, I re - peat: How
C D7 G Gm Go7 G7 C F7 C F7
mf
long has this been go-ing on? Oh, I feel that I could melt;
long has this been go-ing on? Dear, when in your arms I creep,

Cmaj7 F7 Cmaj7 Em6 Bm Em6 Bm Em6
in - to Heav-en I'm hurled! I know how Co - lum - bus felt,
that di - vine ren - dez - vous, don't wake me, if I'm a - sleep,
Bm Em6 Dm Bb+ D7 Do7 Bb
find - ing an - oth - er world! Kiss me once, then once more
let me dream that it's true. Kiss me twice, then once more
mf
D7 D7+5 G7 C7 Cm7 G Go Am7 D7 G7
what a dunce I was be - fore. What a break! For Heav-en's sake! How
that makes thrice, let's make it four! What a break! For Heav-en's sake! How
1. 2.
C D7 G Go C C6 G
long has this been go - ing on?
long has this been go - ing on?
sf

LIZA (All The Clouds'll Roll Away)

Words by
GUS KAHN and IRA GERSHWIN

Music by
GEORGE GERSHWIN

Eb Ebdim Fm7 Abm6 Bb7 Gm7 C7
whis - per sweet and low, That you ought to know, my Li - za!
Ab6 Am6 Eb F7-9
I get lone - some, hon - ey, When I'm all a - lone so long;
Bb Eb Ebm Bb C7 Ebm6 Bb Gm7 Cm7 F9 Bb rall. Fm7 Gm Bb7
Don't make me wait; Don't hes - i - tate; Come and hear my song:
rall.
Refrain Eb
p-mf a tempo.
Bb7 Cdim C7 Abm6 Cdim Bbm6 Eb9
Li - za, Li - za, skies are gray,
a tempo.
p-mf

Ab Fm7 Gm C9 Fm Bb7
But if you'll smile on me All the clouds-'ll roll a -
Eb Ab Eb Fm7 Eb Bb7 Cdim C7 Ab Cdim
way. Li - za, Li - za, don't de -
Bbm6 Eb9 Ab Fm7 Gm C9 Fm Bb7
lay, Come, keep me com - pa - ny, And the clouds-'ll roll a -
Eb G7+5 G7 mf C C7 Cdim G7 Cm
way. See the hon - ey - moon a - shin - in'
mf

Gdim Eb7 Ab Fm Bbm7 Eb7
down; We should make a date with
Ab6 Ab Ebm6 Bb7 Eb Bb7 Cdim C7
Par - son Brown. So, Li - za, Li - za,
fp
Abm6 Cdim Bbm6 Eb9 Ab Fm7 Gm C9
name the day When you be - long to me
Fm Bb7 1 Eb Db Bm7 Bb7 2 Eb
And the clouds-'ll roll a - way. - way.
Ped. *

I'VE GOT A CRUSH ON YOU

Music and Lyrics by
GEORGE GERSHWIN
and IRA GERSHWIN

D A7 D
wore down my re - sist - ance: I fell, and it was swell.
Cm7 F7(6) B♭ B♭dim Cm7 F7 B♭6 Cm7 F7
She: You're my big and brave and hand - some Ro - me - o. How I
B♭ Bmaj.7 B♭6 C7(6) F7 B♭
won you I shall nev - er, nev - er know. He: It's not that you're at - trac - tive, But

Gm7 C7 F9 Cm7-5 F7
oh my heart grew ac-tive when you came in-to view.
Refrain
Bbmaj.7 Bbdim Cm7 F7
He: I've got a crush on you, Sweet-ie Pie.
She: I've got a crush on you, Sweet-ie Pie.
mp
Bbmaj.7 Bbdim Cm7 F7 Bb Bbmaj.7
All the day and night-time hear me sigh. I nev-er had
All the day and night-time hear me sigh. This is-n't just
mf
Gm7 C9 C7 Gm7 C9 C7
the least no-tion that I could fall with so much e-
a flir-ta-tion: We're prov-ing that there's pre-des-ti-

F9 Bbmaj.7 Bbdim Cm7
mo - tion. Could you coo, Could you care
na - tion. I could coo, I could care
mp
F7 Bbmaj.7 Bbdim Cm7 Daug.5(b9) D7
for a cun-ning cot - tage we could share? The
for that cun-ning cot - tage we could share. Your
Gm7 C7 Bbmaj.7 Bb C9 C#dim C9
world will par - don my mush, 'Cause I've got a crush, my ba-
mush I nev - er shall shush, 'Cause I've got a crush, my ba-
sf
mf
F#m7 F7 1. Bb Em7-5 Cm7 F7 2. Bb Em7-5 F7 Bb
- by, on you. I've got a
- by, on you.
mf
fz

SOON

Music and Lyrics by
GEORGE GERSHWIN
and IRA GERSHWIN

Cm7-5 F9 B♭ F7 Gm Dm
fast. The man - y lone - ly nights and days when this duf - fer
E♭ B♭ C7 B♭
just had to suf - fer, are past. She: Life will be a
F9-5 F9 B♭ B♭7 B♭7+5
poco rit.
dream song, love will be the theme song.
poco rit.
Not fast with tender expression
E♭ Cm7-5 Gm7-5
Refrain:
He: Soon the lone - ly nights will be
She: Soon, my dear, you'll nev - er be
p-f

C7+5 C7 Fm C7 Fm7-5
end - ed, soon, two hearts as one will be
lone - ly, soon, you'll find I live for you
Bb7+5 Bb7 Eb Bb7 Eb Eb7 Cm Eb7+5 Ab6
blend - ed. I've found the hap - pi - ness I've wait - ed for;
on - ly. When I'm with you who cares what time it is,
L.H. poco rit.
a tempo
Fm C7 Fm Dm7-5 G7 Cm7
the on - ly girl that I was fat - ed for.
or what the place or what the cli - mate is?
poco rit.
a tempo
Fm7 Bb7 Eb Cm7-5 Gm7-5
Oh, soon a lit - tle cot - tage will
Oh, soon our lit - tle ship will come
mp

C7+5 C7 Fm C7+5 Fm7-5
find us safe with all our cares far be-
sail - ing home through ev - 'ry storm, nev - er
Bb7+5 Bb7 Eb Bb7 Eb Eb7 Eb7+5
hind us; the day your mine this world will
fail ing; the day your mine this world will
L.H. poco rit.
Ab Fm7-5 Eb Ab6 Bb7
be in tune, let's make that day come
be in tune, let's make that day come
mf a tempo p
1. Eb B7 Bb7 2. Eb
soon. soon.
mf 3 dim.

BIDIN' MY TIME

Music and Lyrics by
GEORGE GERSHWIN
and IRA GERSHWIN

Gmin. Gmin. add E D7 with G D7 G B♭7
Some fel-lers must go "Swing-in' Down The Lane." But
Refrain
p-mf
E♭ A♭ F min.7 B♭7 E♭ A♭
I'm Bid-in' My Time; 'Cause that's the kind-a guy
I'm Bid-in' My Time; 'Cause that's the kind-a guy
F min.7 B♭7 E♭ C7 Fmin.7 A♭min. add F
I'm, While oth-er folks grow diz-zy I keep bus-y
I'm. Be-gin-nin' on a Mon-day Right through Sun-day,
E♭ B♭7 E♭ mp G7 C G7 C
Bid-in' My Time. Next year, next year,
Bid-in' My Time. Give me, give me

G7 F C mf Bb7 Eb Bb7 Eb
Some-thin's bound to hap - pen; - This year, - this year, -
Glass that's full of tink - le, - Let me, - let me -
C min.7 open Eb min. add C F7 Bb7 with Eb Bb7 p Eb Ab
I'll just keep on nap - pin,' - And Bid - in' - My
Dream like Rip Van Wink - le. - - He Bid - ed His
F min.7 Bb7 Eb Ab F min.7 Bb7 Eb C7
time - 'Cause that's the kind-a guy I'm. - There's no re - gret-tin'
time. - And like that Wink-le guy I'm - - Chas - in' 'way flies,
mf F min.7 Ab min. add F Eb Bb7 1. Eb Bb7 2 Eb
When I'm set - tin' Bid - in' My Time. - Time. -
How the day flies, Bid - in' My

BUT NOT FOR ME

Music and Lyrics by
GEORGE GERSHWIN
and IRA GERSHWIN

G D+ Dm C+ Eb+ Bm Db+ Am D7
Bea - trice Fair - fax, don't you dare Ev - er tell me he will care; I'm
l. h.
Em7 D7 G F# G Eo
cer - tain It's the fi - nal cur - tain, I nev - er want to
Fm7 Bb7 Ab Bb7 Cm6
hear From an - y cheer - ful Pol - ly - an - nas, Who tell you
Fm7 Bb7 Cm7 Bb7 Eb Bb7
fate, Sup - plies a mate; It's all ba - na - nas! They're writ - ing
(He's knock - ing)

Refrain:
Rather slow (smoothly)
p-mf
Eb Bb7 Cm7 Bb7 Eb Bb7 Eb Bb7 Eb Bb7
songs of love, But not for me. A luck - y
on a door, But not for me. He'll plan a
F7 Bb7 Eb7
star's a - bove, But not for me. With love to
two by four, But not for me. I know that
Eb+ Ab Fm7 F#° Eb Cm Bb7 Eb
lead the way I've found more clouds of gray Than an - y
love's a game; I'm puz - zled, just the same, Was I the
Eb+ Fm7 Fm6 F7-5 Bb7 Eb Bb7
Rus - sian play Could guar - an - tee. I was a
moth or flame? I'm all at sea. It all be -

Eb Bb7 Cm7 Bb7 Eb Bb7 Eb Bb7 Eb Bb7 F7
fool to fall And get that way; Heigh-ho! A-las! and al-
gan so well, But what an end! This is the time a fell-
Bb7 Eb7 Ab+ Eb7 Eb+ Ab
so, Lack-a-day! Al-though I can't dis-miss
er needs a friend, When ev-'ry hap-py plot
Fm7 Cm Fm F#o Eb G7 Cm C7+5 Fm7
The mem-'ry of his kiss, I guess he's not
Ends with the mar-riage knot, And there's no knot
dim.
Bb7 Eb Am6 Fm A7 Bb Eb Bb7 Eb Do Eb
1. 2.
for me. He's knock-ing
for me.

EMBRACEABLE YOU

Music and Lyrics by
GEORGE GERSHWIN
and IRA GERSHWIN

G
What was it that con - trolled ___ me?
F♯7
What kept my love - life
B
lean?
F♯7
My in - tu - i - tion told ___
B
me You'd come
Am7
on
G
the scene.
La - dy,
Em A9 Em A9
lis - ten to the rhy - thm of my
Em Em6 Em A7
heart - beat, And you'll
Am D
rall. e dim.
get just what I
Am D Am D Am D
mean.
rall. e dim.

Rhythmically
Refrain:
G C#o D7 Am11 Fm6 D7
Em - brace me, My sweet em - brace - a - ble you!
p - mf
Am F7 D7 G D7sus4 G
Em - brace me, You ir - re - place - a - ble you!
Em Em7 Em6 F#7 Bm Bb+ Bm7 E7
Just one look at you, my heart grew tip - sy in me;
D D#o A7 D7
You and you a - lone bring out the gyp - sy in me!

G C#o D7 C Fm6 D7
I love all the man - y charms a - bout you;
Am F7 D7 G7 D7sus4 Bbm6 G7 C
A - bove all I want my arms a - bout you.
Don't be a
Am6 B7 Em Eb+ G Em6 G
naught - y ba - by, Come to pa - pa, Come to pa - pa, do!
My sweet em -
L.H.
Cm6 D 1. G Eb A D7 2. G
brace - a - ble you! you!

I GOT RHYTHM

Music and Lyrics by
GEORGE GERSHWIN
and IRA GERSHWIN

Cm Gm6 Eb7 Gm Gm7
tree sing Their day - ful of song, Why should - n't
Cm7 F7 Bb Fm7 Bb Fm7 Bb D D7
we sing a - long? I'm chip - per
Faug5 D7 Cm7 Eb7 D D7
all the day, Hap - py with my lot. How do I
Faug5 D7 Cm7 F7 Edim Gb7 F7 Bbm6 Ddim F7
get that way? Look at what I've got:
sf

REFRAIN *(with abandon)*

Fm6 D7 G Daug5 Dm G7 C7 Gm7 Ebm6 C9
Troub - le, I don't mind him, You won't find him
C7-5 F7 C7 F7 Bb Bb6 Cm7 F7 Bb6 Edim
'Round my door. I got star - light, I got
Cm7 F7 Bb Bb6 Cm7 F7 Ebm Bb Fm
sweet dreams, I got my man Who could ask for an - y-thing
G7 C7 F7 1. Bb Ab Gb Db 2. Bb
more, Who could ask for an - y-thing more? more?
sfz

OF THEE I SING
(BABY)

Music and Lyrics by
GEORGE GERSHWIN
and IRA GERSHWIN

mp
G Am7 G Am7 G D7 sus.4
You're the dream girl of the sweet - est sto - ry ev - er
mp
G D7 sus.4 D7 Gma.7
told, A dream I've sought, Both night and day For years through
C7 sus.4 C7 F B7
all the U. S. A. The star I've hitched my wag - on
Em Am7 D7 Dm G7
to Is ver - y ob - vi - ous - ly you.
poco rit

Refrain
slowly and with expression
C C7+5 F Dm G7
Of thee I sing, ba - by,
C Cma.7 C7 Dm Fm
Sum-mer, Au-tumn, Win - ter, Spring, ba - by,
C Caug5 Am Am7 D7 G
You're my sil - ver lin - ing, You're my sky of blue;
Em Cm G D7 G B♭m D7 G7
There's a love light shin - ing, Just be-cause of you.

C C7+5 F Dm G7 C
mp
Of thee I sing, ba - by, You have got that
mp
C7+5 Dm poco a poco cresc. E7 Am E7 Am Edim Dm Edim7 Dm
cer - tain thing, ba - by! Shin - ing star and in - spi - ra - tion
poco a poco cresc.
mf Am E7 Am Edim7 Dm Edim7 Dm Cdim7 C Am7 Dm G7
Worth - y of a might - y na - tion Of thee I
mf
più f ed espr.
pesante
1. C 2. C
sing. sing.
f

WHO CARES?
(SO LONG AS YOU CARE FOR ME)

Music and Lyrics by
GEORGE GERSHWIN
and IRA GERSHWIN

D♭ Dm G7 Am7 Dm Am7 B7 Em
Stocks and bonds that I've been burned with. I love you and
Am Em Am G
you love me And that's how it will al-ways be, And noth-ing else can
Am7 D7 F G7 F, G7 C9 C C9 C A♭7 D7-5
ev-er mean a thing. Who cares what the pub-lic
G B♭m Cm G C9 C C9 C A♭7 D7-5 G G7 Em G7
chat-ters? Love's the on-ly thing that mat-ters. Who
poco rall.
poco rall.

Refrain
(in a lilting manner)
p-mf
melody well pronounced
C7 G+5 C+5 E7 F+5 A7 Fm Fm
cares If the sky cares to fall in the sea? Who
Who
C Dm Em Co7 Dm7 Em G7
cares What banks fail in Yonkers?
cares How his - to - ry rates me?
C G7 Am7 E7 Am Ab7 D+5 G7
Long as you've got a kiss that con - quers,
Long as your kiss in - tox - i - cates me!

mp
C7 G+5 C+5 E7
Why should I care? Life is
mp ben cantando
Am D7 Ab7 mf C
one long ju - bi - lee, So long as I care
mf
C°7 Dm7 Em A7 Dm G7
2nd time optional
for you And you care for
1 2
C G7 C
me. Who me.
f

ISN'T IT A PITY

From "Pardon My English"

Music and Lyrics by
GEORGE GERSHWIN
and IRA GERSHWIN

F G7 G7/F C/E B7 Bb7 A7
cresc.
rhyme? Is - n't it a pit - y? Is - n't it a crime?
-rive — All my Dres - den boy friends Were on - ly half a - live.
D9 Dm7-5
My jour - ney's end - ed; Ev - 'ry - thing is splen - did:
Sleep - y was Her - mann, Fritz was like a ser - mon,
C F#m7-5/A B7 Em Am
Meet - ing you to - day Has giv - en me a
Hans was such a bore! How well you planned it!
Em7 A7 D7sus4 D7 G7 G7+5
Won - der - ful i - dea, — Here I stay!
I just could - n't stand it An - y more!

p-mf not fast, with expression
C Em7 F B7+5 Em A7
It's a fun-ny thing, I look at you — I get a thrill
con calore
p-mf
Dm G7 C C9/E F C/E Dm7 G11
I nev-er knew, — Is-n't it a pit-y we nev-er met — be-
C/E A°7 G7 C Em7
fore? Here we are at last!
F B7+5 Em A7 Dm7 G7
It's like a dream! The two of us — A per-fect team!

C C9/E F C/E Dm7 G11 C Dm7 G7
Is-n't it a pit-y we nev-er met be-fore?
C Dm9 Am6 Em/B Em F♯11 B7
mf
Im-ag-ine all the lone-ly years we've wast-ed:
Im-ag-ine all the lone-ly years you've wast-ed:
mf
Em A7 G6/D G
You, with the neigh-bors,— I, at sil-ly la-bors; What joys un-
Fish-ing for sal-mon, Los-ing at back-gam-mon. What joys un-
Am7 D7 G7 F9+11 F7
tast-ed! You, read-ing Hei-ne, I, some-where in Chin-a.
tast-ed! My nights were sour_ Spent with Scho-pen-hau-er.

C Em7 F B7+5
Hap - pi - est of men I'm sure to be,
Let's for - get the past Let's both a - gree
Em A7 Dm G7
If on - ly you will say to me,
That I'm for you And you're for me,
C C9+5 Fmaj7 Em7 Dm7 G9
"It's an aw - ful pit - y, We nev - er, nev - er met be -
And it's such a pit - y, We nev - er, nev - er met be -
ten.
ten.
C Dm7 G7 G7+5 C C7+5 G7 C
fore." fore."
mf
sf

MINE

Music and Lyrics by
GEORGE GERSHWIN
and IRA GERSHWIN

Mine - 7 - 1

Am
Wor-ried to-geth-er, Strug-gled to-geth-er,
F7 E
Stood to-geth-er, to-geth-er,
F+ Dm F+ Dm
I grow so sen-ti-men-tal,
espr.
Ab
recit.
I'm a-fraid I've got to burst in-to
sfp
G Am7
song. All: Please
mf
Dm Em Dm7 Dm Em Am7
do. We'd love to know how you
G7 Am7 G7 Em7 Am Dm7 Em7
feel a-bout her, And how she feels a-bout
Dm B7-5
you.

Slowly, with much expression
1st Refrain:
Am F+ D7 G+ Am F+ D7 G+
Mine, love is mine, Wheth - er it
3
p legato
Am F+ D7 G+ Am G+ Gm E° C7
rain or storm or shine.
Dm Bb+ G7 C C+ Dm Bb+ G7 C+
Mine, you are mine, Nev - er an -
Dm Am Dm Am Dm Dm7 G7 Fm Am F7
oth - er Val - en - tine. And I am

Am F+ D7 G+ Am F+ D7 G+
mp
yours, Tell me that I'm yours, Show me that
mp
rubato
3
Am F+ D7 G+ Am G+ Gm E° C7
smile My heart a - dores.
F E E♭ D7 Em B7 E7 A7
3
Mine, more than di - vine, To
Am Dm7 C Am Cm C+ A♭m
know that love like yours is mine.

(1st time counter-melody alone, 2nd time both melodies)
2nd Refrain:
Am F+ D7 G+ Am F+
p
Mine, love is mine,
Patter
p
The point they're mak - ing in the song Is that they more than
p grazioso e leggiero
D7 G+ Am F+ D7 G+
3
Wheth - er it's rain or storm or
get a - long, And he is not a - shamed to say
Am G+ Gm F♯m C7 Dm B♭+ G7 C+
shine. Mine, you are mine,
She made him what he is to - day. It does a per - son good to see

Dm Bb+ G7 C+ Dm Am F Am
Nev-er an-oth - er Val - en-
Such hap-py do-mes - tic-i-ty, The way they're mak-ing love, you'd swear
G7 Am Dm G7 Fm Am F7 Am F+ D7 G+
tine. And I am yours, Tell me that I'm
They're not a mar-ried pair, He says no mat-ter what oc-curs,
mf
p
Am F+ D7 G+ Am F+ D7 G+
yours, Show me that smile, My heart a-
What-ev-er he may have is hers, The point that she is mak-ing is

Am G+ Gm F#m C7 F E Eb D7
dores. Mine, more than di -
What - ev - er she may have is his. Mine more than di -
3
Em B7 E7 A7 Am Dm7
vine, To know that love like yours is
vine, To know that love like yours is
1. 2.
C Am Cm C+ Abm C
mine. mine.
mine. mine.
f

BY STRAUSS

Music and Lyrics by
GEORGE GERSHWIN
and IRA GERSHWIN

Dm6 E7 Cm6 D7
Oh, I'd give no quar - ter to Kern or Cole Por - ter and
Bb m6 C9 F Gm
Gersh-win keeps pound-ing on tin. How can I be
Fmaj7 Gm
civ - il when hear - ing this driv - el? It's on - ly for
Dm6 Bb m6 F Fmaj7 F6 E9
night club-bing sous - es. Oh, give me the free 'n' eas - y
mf

Am7
Am6
C
D9
C
waltz that is Vi-en-nese-y And go tell the band if
G7
C
they want a hand the waltz must be Strauss's!
Bb
Bbm
C7
Bb
Ya, ya, ya! Give me
mp grazioso
Am
Abm
C7
oom - pah - pah!
f marcato

Refrain:
Gm7 C9 F
When I want a mel-o-dy lilt-ing through the house,
mp-mf a tempo
Gm7 C7 C9+5 F6 Dm6
Then I want a mel-o-dy By Strauss! It
E7 Em7 A7 Am7 D7 Gm Dm7
laughs! it sings! The world is in rhyme, Swing-ing to
G7 G7-5 C7 Gm7 C9 B♭m
three quar-ter time. Let the "Da-nube" flow a-long And the "Fle-der-
fp
a tempo

F Gm7 C7 C9+5 F6
maus!" Keep the wine and give me song By Strauss!
F7 Bb Db Eb F Fdim
By Jo! By Jing! "By Strauss" is the thing! So I say to
mf animato
mp calmo
Gm7 C9 C7+5 F F7 D7 Gm
ha-cha-cha Her - aus! Just give me a oom-pah-pah
C7 C11 1. F Db7 C7 2. F C9 F
By Strauss. When I want a Strauss.
mf
sf

THE FRENCH DOLL 1922
Do It Again

GEORGE WHITE'S SCANDALS 1922
I'll Build A Stairway To Paradise

GEORGE WHITE'S SCANDALS 1924
Somebody Loves Me

LADY, BE GOOD 1924
Fascinating Rhythm
The Man I Love
Oh, Lady Be Good

TIP-TOES 1925
Sweet And Low-Down

OH, KAY 1926
Clap 'Yo Hands
Fidgety Feet
Someone To Watch Over Me

STRIKE UP THE BAND 1927
Strike Up The Band

FUNNY FACE 1927
The Babbit And The Bromide
Funny Face
He Loves And She Loves
High Hat
My One And Only
'S Wonderful

ROSALIE 1928
How Long Has This Been Going On?

SHOW GIRL 1929
Liza

STRIKE UP THE BAND 1930
I've Got A Crush On You
Soon
Strike Up The Band

GIRL CRAZY 1930
Bidin' My Time
But Not For Me
Embraceable You
I Got Rhythm

OF THEE I SING 1931
Of Thee I Sing
Who Cares?

PARDON MY ENGLISH 1933
Isn't It A Pity

LET 'EM EAT CAKE 1933
Mine

THE SHOW IS ON 1936
By Strauss